MW00887185

This wonderful journal
of memories belongs to:

_____

CREATIVE NOTEBOOKS

We would love to hear from you! Connect with us at:

✉ info@creativenotebooks.com

↖ www.creativenotebooks.com

📘 facebook.com/creativenotebooks

📷 instagram.com/creative.notebooks

Copyright © Creative Notebooks

In no way is it legal to reproduce, duplicate, or transmit any part of this document in either electronic means or in printed format. Copying this publication is strictly prohibited and any replication of this document is not allowed unless with written permission from the publisher. All rights reserved.

Who said it?: _____

When was it said?: _____

What was their age?: _____

Where was it said?: _____

Who said it?: _____

When was it said?: _____

What was their age?: _____

Where was it said?: _____

Who said it?: _____

When was it said?: _____

What was their age?: _____

Where was it said?: _____

Who said it?: _____

When was it said?: _____

What was their age?: _____

Where was it said?: _____

"

"

Who said it?: _____

When was it said?: _____

What was their age?: _____

Where was it said?: _____

Who said it?: _____

When was it said?: _____

What was their age?: _____

Where was it said?: _____

Who said it?: _____

When was it said?: _____

What was their age?: _____

Where was it said?: _____

Who said it?: _____

When was it said?: _____

What was their age?: _____

Where was it said?: _____

Who said it?: _____

When was it said?: _____

What was their age?: _____

Where was it said?: _____

Who said it?: _____

When was it said?: _____

What was their age?: _____

Where was it said?: _____

Who said it?: _____

When was it said?: _____

What was their age?: _____

Where was it said?: _____

Who said it?: _____

When was it said?: _____

What was their age?: _____

Where was it said?: _____

Who said it?: _____

When was it said?: _____

What was their age?: _____

Where was it said?: _____

Who said it?: _____

When was it said?: _____

What was their age?: _____

Where was it said?: _____

Who said it?: _____

When was it said?: _____

What was their age?: _____

Where was it said?: _____

Who said it?: _____

When was it said?: _____

What was their age?: _____

Where was it said?: _____

Who said it?: _____

When was it said?: _____

What was their age?: _____

Where was it said?: _____

Who said it?: _____

When was it said?: _____

What was their age?: _____

Where was it said?: _____

Who said it?: _____

When was it said?: _____

What was their age?: _____

Where was it said?: _____

Who said it?: _____

When was it said?: _____

What was their age?: _____

Where was it said?: _____

Who said it?: _____

When was it said?: _____

What was their age?: _____

Where was it said?: _____

Who said it?: _____

When was it said?: _____

What was their age?: _____

Where was it said?: _____

Who said it?: _____

When was it said?: _____

What was their age?: _____

Where was it said?: _____

Who said it?: _____

When was it said?: _____

What was their age?: _____

Where was it said?: _____

Who said it?: _____

When was it said?: _____

What was their age?: _____

Where was it said?: _____

Who said it?: _____

When was it said?: _____

What was their age?: _____

Where was it said?: _____

Who said it?: _____

When was it said?: _____

What was their age?: _____

Where was it said?: _____

Who said it?: _____

When was it said?: _____

What was their age?: _____

Where was it said?: _____

Who said it?: _____

When was it said?: _____

What was their age?: _____

Where was it said?: _____

Who said it?: _____

When was it said?: _____

What was their age?: _____

Where was it said?: _____

Who said it?: _____

When was it said?: _____

What was their age?: _____

Where was it said?: _____

Who said it?: _____

When was it said?: _____

What was their age?: _____

Where was it said?: _____

Who said it?: _____

When was it said?: _____

What was their age?: _____

Where was it said?: _____

Who said it?: _____

When was it said?: _____

What was their age?: _____

Where was it said?: _____

Who said it?: _____

When was it said?: _____

What was their age?: _____

Where was it said?: _____

Who said it?: _____

When was it said?: _____

What was their age?: _____

Where was it said?: _____

Who said it?: _____

When was it said?: _____

What was their age?: _____

Where was it said?: _____

Who said it?: _____

When was it said?: _____

What was their age?: _____

Where was it said?: _____

Who said it?: _____

When was it said?: _____

What was their age?: _____

Where was it said?: _____

Who said it?: _____

When was it said?: _____

What was their age?: _____

Where was it said?: _____

Who said it?: _____

When was it said?: _____

What was their age?: _____

Where was it said?: _____

Who said it?: _____

When was it said?: _____

What was their age?: _____

Where was it said?: _____

Who said it?: _____

When was it said?: _____

What was their age?: _____

Where was it said?: _____

Who said it?: _____

When was it said?: _____

What was their age?: _____

Where was it said?: _____

Who said it?: _____

When was it said?: _____

What was their age?: _____

Where was it said?: _____

Who said it?: _____

When was it said?: _____

What was their age?: _____

Where was it said?: _____

Who said it?: _____

When was it said?: _____

What was their age?: _____

Where was it said?: _____

Who said it?: _____

When was it said?: _____

What was their age?: _____

Where was it said?: _____

Who said it?: _____

When was it said?: _____

What was their age?: _____

Where was it said?: _____

Who said it?: _____

When was it said?: _____

What was their age?: _____

Where was it said?: _____

Who said it?: _____

When was it said?: _____

What was their age?: _____

Where was it said?: _____

Who said it?: _____

When was it said?: _____

What was their age?: _____

Where was it said?: _____

Who said it?: _____

When was it said?: _____

What was their age?: _____

Where was it said?: _____

Who said it?: _____

When was it said?: _____

What was their age?: _____

Where was it said?: _____

Who said it?: _____

When was it said?: _____

What was their age?: _____

Where was it said?: _____

Who said it?: _____

When was it said?: _____

What was their age?: _____

Where was it said?: _____

Who said it?: _____

When was it said?: _____

What was their age?: _____

Where was it said?: _____

Who said it?: _____

When was it said?: _____

What was their age?: _____

Where was it said?: _____

Who said it?: _____

When was it said?: _____

What was their age?: _____

Where was it said?: _____

Who said it?: _____

When was it said?: _____

What was their age?: _____

Where was it said?: _____

Who said it?: _____

When was it said?: _____

What was their age?: _____

Where was it said?: _____

Who said it?: _____

When was it said?: _____

What was their age?: _____

Where was it said?: _____

Who said it?: _____

When was it said?: _____

What was their age?: _____

Where was it said?: _____

Who said it?: _____

When was it said?: _____

What was their age?: _____

Where was it said?: _____

Who said it?: _____

When was it said?: _____

What was their age?: _____

Where was it said?: _____

Who said it?: _____

When was it said?: _____

What was their age?: _____

Where was it said?: _____

Who said it?: _____

When was it said?: _____

What was their age?: _____

Where was it said?: _____

Who said it? : _____

When was it said? : _____

What was their age? : _____

Where was it said? : _____

"

"

Who said it?: _____

When was it said?: _____

What was their age?: _____

Where was it said?: _____

Who said it?: _____

When was it said?: _____

What was their age?: _____

Where was it said?: _____

Who said it?: _____

When was it said?: _____

What was their age?: _____

Where was it said?: _____

Who said it?: _____

When was it said?: _____

What was their age?: _____

Where was it said?: _____

Who said it?: _____

When was it said?: _____

What was their age?: _____

Where was it said?: _____

Who said it?: _____

When was it said?: _____

What was their age?: _____

Where was it said?: _____

Who said it?: _____

When was it said?: _____

What was their age?: _____

Where was it said?: _____

Who said it?: _____

When was it said?: _____

What was their age?: _____

Where was it said?: _____

Who said it?: _____

When was it said?: _____

What was their age?: _____

Where was it said?: _____

Who said it?: _____

When was it said?: _____

What was their age?: _____

Where was it said?: _____

Who said it?: _____

When was it said?: _____

What was their age?: _____

Where was it said?: _____

Who said it?: _____

When was it said?: _____

What was their age?: _____

Where was it said?: _____

Who said it?: _____

When was it said?: _____

What was their age?: _____

Where was it said?: _____

Who said it?: _____

When was it said?: _____

What was their age?: _____

Where was it said?: _____

Who said it?: _____

When was it said?: _____

What was their age?: _____

Where was it said?: _____

Who said it?: _____

When was it said?: _____

What was their age?: _____

Where was it said?: _____

Who said it?: _____

When was it said?: _____

What was their age?: _____

Where was it said?: _____

Who said it?: _____

When was it said?: _____

What was their age?: _____

Where was it said?: _____

Who said it?: _____

When was it said?: _____

What was their age?: _____

Where was it said?: _____

Who said it?: _____

When was it said?: _____

What was their age?: _____

Where was it said?: _____

Who said it?: _____

When was it said?: _____

What was their age?: _____

Where was it said?: _____

Who said it?: _____

When was it said?: _____

What was their age?: _____

Where was it said?: _____

"

„„

Who said it?: _____

When was it said?: _____

What was their age?: _____

Where was it said?: _____

Who said it?: _____

When was it said?: _____

What was their age?: _____

Where was it said?: _____

Who said it?: _____

When was it said?: _____

What was their age?: _____

Where was it said?: _____

Who said it?: _____

When was it said?: _____

What was their age?: _____

Where was it said?: _____

Who said it?: _____

When was it said?: _____

What was their age?: _____

Where was it said?: _____

Who said it?: _____

When was it said?: _____

What was their age?: _____

Where was it said?: _____

"

"

Who said it?: _____

When was it said?: _____

What was their age?: _____

Where was it said?: _____

Who said it?: _____

When was it said?: _____

What was their age?: _____

Where was it said?: _____

Who said it?: _____

When was it said?: _____

What was their age?: _____

Where was it said?: _____

"

„

Who said it?: _____

When was it said?: _____

What was their age?: _____

Where was it said?: _____

Who said it?: _____

When was it said?: _____

What was their age?: _____

Where was it said?: _____

Who said it?: _____

When was it said?: _____

What was their age?: _____

Where was it said?: _____

Who said it?: _____

When was it said?: _____

What was their age?: _____

Where was it said?: _____

Who said it?: _____

When was it said?: _____

What was their age?: _____

Where was it said?: _____

Who said it?: _____

When was it said?: _____

What was their age?: _____

Where was it said?: _____

Who said it?: _____

When was it said?: _____

What was their age?: _____

Where was it said?: _____

Who said it?: _____

When was it said?: _____

What was their age?: _____

Where was it said?: _____

Who said it?: _____

When was it said?: _____

What was their age?: _____

Where was it said?: _____

Who said it?: _____

When was it said?: _____

What was their age?: _____

Where was it said?: _____

Who said it?: _____

When was it said?: _____

What was their age?: _____

Where was it said?: _____

Who said it?: _____

When was it said?: _____

What was their age?: _____

Where was it said?: _____

Who said it?: _____

When was it said?: _____

What was their age?: _____

Where was it said?: _____

Who said it?: _____

When was it said?: _____

What was their age?: _____

Where was it said?: _____

Who said it?: _____

When was it said?: _____

What was their age?: _____

Where was it said?: _____

Who said it?: _____

When was it said?: _____

What was their age?: _____

Where was it said?: _____

Who said it?: _____

When was it said?: _____

What was their age?: _____

Where was it said?: _____

Who said it?: _____

When was it said?: _____

What was their age?: _____

Where was it said?: _____

Who said it?: _____

When was it said?: _____

What was their age?: _____

Where was it said?: _____

Who said it?: _____

When was it said?: _____

What was their age?: _____

Where was it said?: _____

Who said it?: _____

When was it said?: _____

What was their age?: _____

Where was it said?: _____

Who said it?: _____

When was it said?: _____

What was their age?: _____

Where was it said?: _____

Who said it?: _____

When was it said?: _____

What was their age?: _____

Where was it said?: _____

Who said it?: _____

When was it said?: _____

What was their age?: _____

Where was it said?: _____

Who said it?: _____

When was it said?: _____

What was their age?: _____

Where was it said?: _____

Who said it?: _____

When was it said?: _____

What was their age?: _____

Where was it said?: _____

Who said it?: _____

When was it said?: _____

What was their age?: _____

Where was it said?: _____

Who said it?: _____

When was it said?: _____

What was their age?: _____

Where was it said?: _____

Who said it?: _____

When was it said?: _____

What was their age?: _____

Where was it said?: _____

Who said it?: _____

When was it said?: _____

What was their age?: _____

Where was it said?: _____

"

"

Who said it?: _____

When was it said?: _____

What was their age?: _____

Where was it said?: _____

Who said it?: _____

When was it said?: _____

What was their age?: _____

Where was it said?: _____

Who said it?: _____

When was it said?: _____

What was their age?: _____

Where was it said?: _____

Who said it?: _____

When was it said?: _____

What was their age?: _____

Where was it said?: _____

Who said it?: _____

When was it said?: _____

What was their age?: _____

Where was it said?: _____

Who said it?: _____

When was it said?: _____

What was their age?: _____

Where was it said?: _____

Who said it?: _____

When was it said?: _____

What was their age?: _____

Where was it said?: _____

Who said it?: _____

When was it said?: _____

What was their age?: _____

Where was it said?: _____

Who said it?: _____

When was it said?: _____

What was their age?: _____

Where was it said?: _____

Who said it?: _____

When was it said?: _____

What was their age?: _____

Where was it said?: _____

Who said it?: _____

When was it said?: _____

What was their age?: _____

Where was it said?: _____

Who said it?: _____

When was it said?: _____

What was their age?: _____

Where was it said?: _____

Who said it?: _____

When was it said?: _____

What was their age?: _____

Where was it said?: _____

Who said it?: _____

When was it said?: _____

What was their age?: _____

Where was it said?: _____

Who said it?: _____

When was it said?: _____

What was their age?: _____

Where was it said?: _____

Who said it?: _____

When was it said?: _____

What was their age?: _____

Where was it said?: _____

Who said it?: _____

When was it said?: _____

What was their age?: _____

Where was it said?: _____

Who said it?: _____

When was it said?: _____

What was their age?: _____

Where was it said?: _____

Who said it?: _____

When was it said?: _____

What was their age?: _____

Where was it said?: _____

Who said it?: _____

When was it said?: _____

What was their age?: _____

Where was it said?: _____

50990527R00086

Made in the USA
San Bernardino, CA
10 July 2017